we are more
than
Beautiful

46 Real Teen Girls Speak Out
about Beauty, Happiness, Love and Life

edited by Woody Winfree
illustrated by Elizabeth Lavin

SOURCEBOOKS, INC.®
NAPERVILLE, ILLINOIS

we are more than Beautiful

46 Real Teen Girls Speak Out
about Beauty, Happiness, Love and Life

Published by Sourcebooks, Inc.
P.O. Box 4410, Naperville, Illinois 60567-4410
(630) 961-3900
Fax: (630) 961-2168
www.sourcebooks.com

Library of Congress Cataloging-in-Publication Data

We are beautiful : 46 real teen girls speak out about beauty, happi-
ness, love and life / [edited by] Woody Winfree.
       p. cm.
   ISBN-13: 978-1-4022-953-6
   ISBN-10: 1-4022-0953-3
   1. Teenage girls--Psychology. 2. Feminine beauty (Aesthetics). 3.
Self-esteem in adolescence. I. Winfree, Woody.

HQ798.W24 2006
158.10835'2--dc22

2006019056

Printed and bound in China
LEO 10   9   8   7   6   5   4   3   2   1

With a full heart, I dedicate this
book to Dana Carpenter, my dear
friend, confidant, and, above all,
partner in projects and dreams—no
matter the course of the journey.

Introduction

I know a thing or two about beauty. One is that it is a lot more fun to express our true beauty than to bury it out of sight. And two, getting to a place of being able to do that can be really hard, especially in our media-driven culture.

Everywhere we look—from movie screens to magazine covers to billboards and the sides of buses—women and the ideal of beauty are portrayed in a very narrow, distorted, and one-dimensional perspective: tall, thin, and overly busty with perfect hair, flawless faces, and sparkling-white, shiny teeth. This singular perspective can be downright dangerous for some—resulting in eating disorders, cutting, even suicide—and certainly depressing for most, making us feel like we need "fixing" in order to be beautiful and to get ahead in life.

The truth is, however, that beauty is not measured by the clothes we wear, the style of our hair, or the size of our waists. Beauty is not one size, one look, one color, or one definition. Rather, beauty is an expression of our talents, interests, contributions, thoughts, accomplishments, dreams, and potential to do great things.

If we were encouraged to identify and celebrate what is unique and beautiful about ourselves just the way we are—rather than trying to morph into something that we're not—then we would recognize that we don't need "fixing." That is what this book is all about.

This book is about learning to say "no" to the narrow and distorted view of feminine beauty and "yes" to one that is broader, more inclusive, and diverse—and that includes you. A good way to start this process is to learn from the example of others—from girls just like you. Each girl's story on these pages is specific to her personal experience but, at the same time, offers the opportunity for you to see into the rich well of beauty that is yours to enjoy, celebrate, and carry into the world.

—Woody Winfree

lea

"Do I look fat?" asks the Jennifer Aniston/Calista Flockhart/Gwyneth Paltrow thing. You sigh with a mixture of disgust, awe, and jealousy, because nothing about this girl looks fat. She's tall and slender, and you'd swear she goes to a beauty parlor every morning before school to get her hair and makeup perfected down to the last split end and stray eyelash. She hasn't repeated an outfit all month, and it's pretty likely she won't. Judging by the number of notebooks with her name written inside a heart seen around school, you are not alone in holding this high opinion.

And you? You with the mousy brown hair just recently cut into an unflattering 'do by your aunt, who is under the bizarre impression that she knows how to cut hair. You with the unreasonable mom who won't let you wear makeup—not that you'd know how to apply all those different powders and creams to your naked face anyway.

And those braces! Despite the long-term results that your orthodontist rambles on about, you hate the ugly squares of metal that are glued to your poor, poor teeth. Maybe, just maybe, if you had some of those cute clothes, your appearance could be saved. No, it seems that the latest fashions have eluded your pathetic closet that is filled with bargain buys from JCPenney. And the puberty fairy must have been too tired from granting all the other girls great bodies, because she has never seemed to show up at your house. Perhaps next year she will drop by.

But please, don't be upset. You do have something in common with this girl. You have inner beauty. Okay, I see your point. What is inner beauty? And more important, why the hell is it hiding inside where no one can see it? Is it shy? You figure that if you had beauty inside you, it most certainly would want to come out and show off. Is it trapped? It must be! Trapped by some bone, organ, or other gross thing beneath your freckled skin.

All right, I can see that I have misjudged you. Your level of intelligence exceeds the "inner beauty" bit? Well, then let me tell you a secret about how to be beautiful; let me share some information that's not widely known. I hope you know the risk I'm taking simply by whispering it in your ear. Listen closely...

Pull back your shoulders and lift up your face. Look directly into the eyes of those who speak to you, and smile. Raise your hand high in class and share your thoughts. Laugh, and don't worry so much if you tend to snort. Know that it's okay to wear jeans that you can breathe in.

Were you expecting something more along the lines of a potion or magic spell? Don't be discouraged. Follow my directions and magical things will happen. You just might see your name written in the center of a notebook heart.

i know who i am. music—all different kinds of music—makes me feel good. I love to dance. clothes—from playful to dressy—help me express myself. i love to have fun. there was a time when I didn't want to stand out. i would listen to and wear the same things that everyone else did. now i am happiest when i am with the people who love me and relate to me for who ireally am. i am not perfect, but that's okay. i am not searching to be someone else.

that makes me beautiful. LAYLA

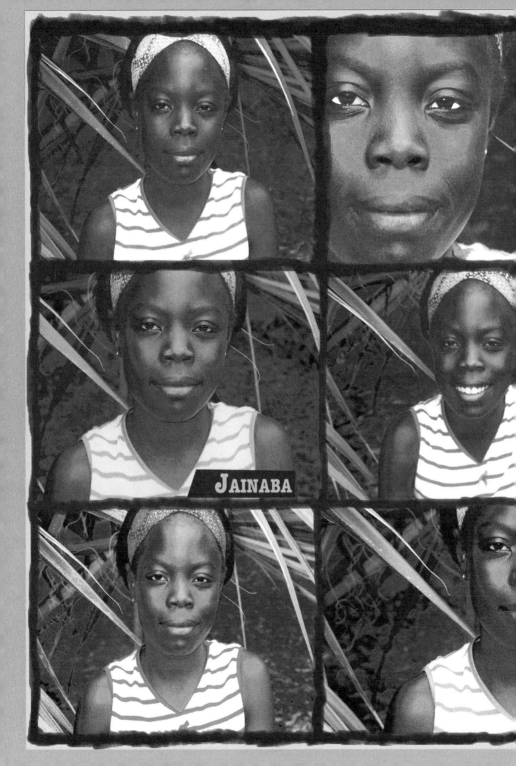

JAINABA

I am beautiful in Africa. Three years ago,
I came to America from Gambia and
people said that I was not beautiful.

I look at myself in the mirror, and I see my
beauty like flowers. At my U.S. school,
some people don't think that I am pretty.
But I do not care. I am beautiful in Africa.

Sometimes I put on makeup. I look in the
mirror and I ask my sister if I am beautiful.
She says, "Yes, you are, Jainaba."

African people are beautiful,
and I am a beautiful girl.

Charlotte

I was diagnosed with bone cancer in my right leg when I was nine.
I went through chemotherapy, lost my hair, and had multiple
surgeries on my leg, which left me with many scars. For a long time
I wouldn't show anybody my scars—not my friends, not my boyfriends.
Nobody saw what I thought as ugly. I never wore shorts or
short skirts or went swimming in public.

One day, my doctor told me about a new laser procedure that would
drastically reduce the appearance of my scars. I was ecstatic at
the thought of finally being rid of them.

That night, as I was lying in bed, I decided that I couldn't do
it. I realized that I had walked through fire to get those scars,
and I wasn't about to let anybody take away such a tangible,
visible reminder of who I am and where I came from.

MOST OF MY CHILDHOOD, I WAS MADE FUN OF FOR BEING "FAT." PEOPLE THOUGHT IT WAS EVEN FUNNIER TO TEASE ME BECAUSE I DIDN'T ACT LIKE IT HURT ME.

I ACTUALLY THOUGHT THAT I WAS PRETTY, BUT I ACTED LIKE THEY WERE RIGHT, WEARING UGLY CLOTHES AND NOT TAKING CARE OF MY APPEARANCE. THEN, IN NINTH GRADE, SOMETHING HAPPENED. I DON'T KNOW WHAT CHANGED, BUT ALL OF A SUDDEN, I STARTED FEELING GOOD ABOUT MYSELF. I STARTED DRESSING BETTER AND MAKING MYSELF LOOK NICE. I GUESS I CAME TO REALIZE THAT BEAUTY HAS A LOT TO DO WITH YOUR PERSONALITY AND THAT I SHOULD BE HAPPY WITH MYSELF. I THINK THAT I LEARNED THAT AS LONG AS I THINK I LOOK GOOD AND FLAUNT THE FACT, THEN PEOPLE WILL THINK THE SAME ABOUT ME. BUT IT DOES TAKE A WHILE FOR BOYS TO NOTICE.

audrey

I am a beautiful runner. Even though I am not fast, when I am running you can tell how much I love it. I think that I show a kind of grace and determination. Running is natural and it takes you to places that you can only imagine in your dreams.

With the arrival of each new season of track and cross-country, so comes a new season of hopes, dreams, tears, joy, pain, frustration, elation, and exhaustion. Endless training leads to a flurry of weekday meets and Saturday invitationals, the former filled with frantic homework and long bus rides into the boonies, the latter requiring us to gather, sometimes just as the sun is rising, in order to travel for hours to compete. On the starting line, the gun goes off. My team and I, we turn into a machine—a spitting, flying, gasping, foaming, cursing, crying, smiling, lunging machine.

Why do I do it? I do it for what I see when I run: sunrises and sunsets; snowflakes falling around me; rabbits, woodchucks, deer, wayward dogs; lightning; frozen puddles of ice. I do it for what I feel: legs that move so effortlessly and fast it almost scares me; painfully pushing myself up a hill while a stream runs beside me in the opposite direction; numb hands in below-freezing temperatures. I do it for the numbers: 15 miles in a day, 47 in one week, 395 miles on one pair of shoes, over 600 in a winter.

I do it because I love it. There is nothing more breathtaking than running at an invitational with over 200 girls, a rainbow of colors. Each one unique—myself included.

Allison

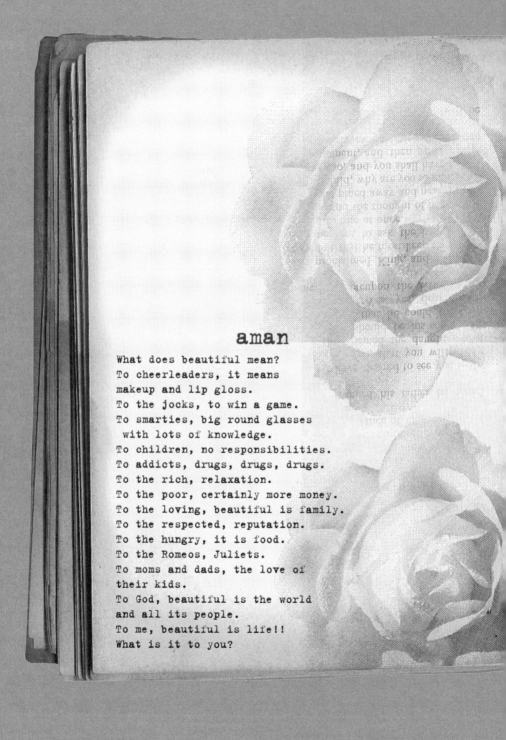

aman

What does beautiful mean?
To cheerleaders, it means
makeup and lip gloss.
To the jocks, to win a game.
To smarties, big round glasses
 with lots of knowledge.
To children, no responsibilities.
To addicts, drugs, drugs, drugs.
To the rich, relaxation.
To the poor, certainly more money.
To the loving, beautiful is family.
To the respected, reputation.
To the hungry, it is food.
To the Romeos, Juliets.
To moms and dads, the love of
their kids.
To God, beautiful is the world
and all its people.
To me, beautiful is life!!
What is it to you?

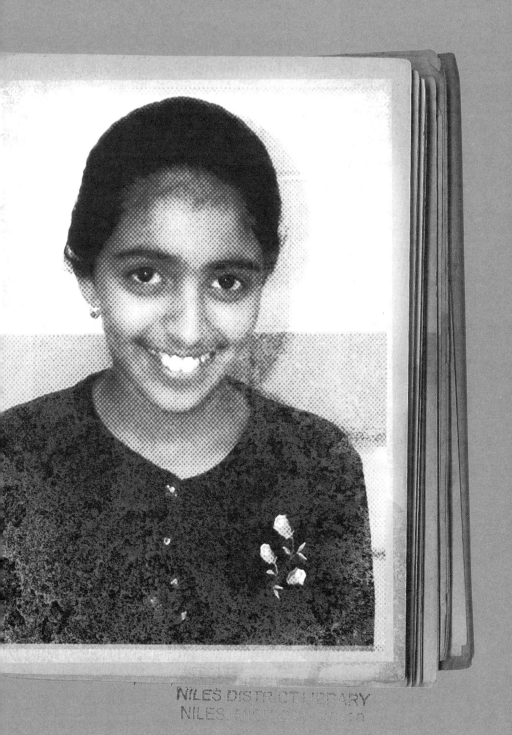

kalie

because my voice is powerful and p

Beauty is a strong word.

Some say beauty is on the inside, and for me, it's really true.Beauty is what I am because my voice is powerful and pure.It can be heard and it reaches out to others. When I sing, I am in a world of my own, and in that world I can accomplish anything. When I sing, it is as if I'm hiking up a mountain, and when I hit the final note, I've reached the top. In my voice I find who I am and nobody can change that. My songs bring joy not only to me, but to others. That is beauty. Pure beauty. That's the voice inside me.

emily

I have been taught the
beauty in living
of life and
living

I am the person I am today because of the many loving adults who surround me. Growing up in a small community, I have often felt as though I have many parents in addition to my biological ones. I have grown up with five other families, all with children my age and my brothers' ages. We six families do a lot together—from monthly potlucks to Thanksgiving cabining trips all over our state. I always feel like a pilgrim when I look down the long picnic tables holding my "family" of twenty-seven people. One mom taught me much about beauty from within; another about the value of being a woman. One dad drove me to school every morning and taught me the importance of taking my time, not rushing or worrying. A mom of four boys taught me strength and patience as I watched her defeat breast cancer. Another dad, with his beautifully handcrafted bowls and furniture, inspired me to add beauty to things that might be merely useful. My own parents showed me how to love myself through their love for me. Growing up among all of these wonderful, strong people, I have been taught the beauty of life and in living.

I am a first-generation Mexican-American girl who, at seventeen years old, fell to the pressures of the media and beauty culture by becoming bulimic. Every time I looked into the mirror, I saw someone so ugly and sad.

To begin with, there is a lot of pressure on minorities to be completely successful in order to be measured as worthwhile. Making things even harder for me was the fact that I was a competitive figure skater for ten years. Our coaches were so harsh, calling us fat cows and comparing us to Michelle Kwan and other famous skaters. There was even one female coach who planted the idea that it was good for us to throw up to get rid of the food we'd eaten.

After about six months of purging, I finally looked inside myself and found someone so strong and lucky to have so many blessings. I realized that I am beautiful because I am such a giving, passionate person. I knew that I could overcome bulimia and I could do anything I wanted in my life.

I took some time off after high school. Now I am a political science major and just made the Dean's list with a 3.5 GPA. I was one of the few from my college to be selected to study in Italy for the spring semester. My plans are to become a foreign diplomat or to run for the U.S. Congress.

SARA

Physical beauty is highly overrated—do you realize how often we teens hear this? Unfortunately, it doesn't have much of an impact. In addition to the numerous stresses of the teen years—such as peer pressure, hormones, and relationships—girls especially have a need to feel beautiful.

We just have to have the perfect nose, stick-straight hair, bold blue eyes, a large bust, and a nonexistent waist. What a lot of us don't process is the fact that none of this matters. We can only realize this through time and maturity. I don't think that the awareness of inner beauty comes in a spontaneous "aha" moment, but rather it is a state of mind that a person just seems to grow into.

This doesn't mean I don't have days when I feel a little unpretty. But I think the point is how I respond to those days. Rather than stressing out or getting depressed, I try to find something productive to do, like call up a friend just to see how he or she is doing; help Mom with the laundry; volunteer at a children's hospital or soup kitchen; or visit my grandparents—just because.

Nicole

Mariah

When I think of who I am, I also think of my mom.
She has been my best teacher yet.
Through her example, I have learned to:
Be myself, speak my mind, and defend my values.
She has taught me how to:
Be the independent woman I'll soon become,
That it's okay to have my own opinions on everything,
And that I can do anything if my heart and mind are set.

She has shown me how to:
Embrace the characteristics that define me,
Feel the power inside me,
And to push myself to meet my goals and reach my dreams.
But most of all, my mom helps me to see that:
I am beautiful,
That beauty comes from within,
And that true beauty is seen without the eye.

*MY EYES ARE CROOKED BUT MY
HEART IS STRAIGHT

dana

My eyes are crooked, but my heart is straight. I am not just made of sugar and spice and everything nice. I'm aggressive at times and at others, an emotional wreck. The favorite parts of my body are my ears, eyes, and arms. My ears to hear my family and friends; my eyes to see their faces; my arms to hug them as much as possible.

I love sports. I play on a tennis team. When I make a point, I turn my face away from my opponent and give the biggest smile! I also run cross-country, lift weights, and am an All-Star cheerleader. I'm not the prettiest girl there is, but I don't need big boobs and a big butt to feel like a woman. Okay, so I like to burp and have farting contests with friends. I hate to shave; it's just so boring. And yet, I am beautiful.

Annamarie

I have an attitude. I am not afraid to let my opinion be known or to tell someone when I don't agree with them. Some people don't like that. I think that is what makes me, me.

When I was a little girl, I had a cyst on my vocal cords, and I could only whisper. In second grade, it disappeared, and I started to get louder. When I was in fourth grade, we had seven people—college students—living in my house, plus all our dogs and cats, and that made me louder. In high school, I was in the drum line, so I got even louder. I like being loud.

I am more than beautiful,
for beauty can be seen as
only skin deep.
When the wind blows,
it is not my hair that dances.
It is my spirit roaming free.
When the sun shines,
it is not my eyes that sparkle.
It is my soul showing through.
I am myself,
not anybody else.
I am proud of that.

(GIRLS SHOUT OUT)

K TX 6043   KODAK

mary

Coming from a "big-boned" family, I knew I would never be small. My American Indian/French Canadian father is 6´4 and weighed 450 pounds at his top. At 6´7, my mother's father was a towering John Wayne look-alike. He was what people call "solid." The family traits I inherited include a sizable figure and dark hair and skin. Living in a small, white, rural farm town in New England, I have always felt different.

At age six, I was wearing a teenager's size 12. In sixth grade, I was wearing a size 18. I always dressed fashionably, just never wearing sizes intended for my age. By my senior year in high school, I weighed 350 pounds. I was almost unaware of having gotten so big, because I was too swamped working on my senior project: coordinating with the plus-size women's magazine *Mode* to produce a benefit fashion show.

But I knew my health, not just my self-esteem, was suffering due to my weight. So, I cracked down and have lost seventy pounds so far. Although I have always had self-esteem, it is even stronger now because I feel better about myself. I am accomplishing my goals, albeit slowly.

Being beautiful starts inside and flows outward. No one can tell me that I am not beautiful. That is for me to decide. Whenever anyone asked me what I wanted to be when I grew up, I always said I wanted to be an icon—be it in the fashion industry or teaching self-acceptance through fashion. Maybe someday I will be.

Brett

romy

I don't think I am beautiful—I know that I am. I am surrounded by beauty—I see it in nature, family, friends, and the love of the community I live in. I'm not the girly-girl type, but sports and my athleticism help me feel my full beauty. When I am out surfing, I feel complete. Sitting out in the ocean on my board waiting for the perfect wave, I am at peace with myself.

i am an unusual girl

while my family is as ordinary, in a nice way, as can be. So how did I get to be so atypical? Maybe it's because I'm almost seventeen years old and I still have no idea what real beauty is. Or maybe it's because I'm just weird. Either way, my individuality is just one of the things that makes me beautiful. Possibly even gorgeous. Just kidding? I don't know. For teenage girls especially, being beautiful means being an Ultra. Ultra-pretty, ultra-popular, ultra-thin, and all that junk. But being beautiful as a personal statement is something else completely. To me, beauty is letting your colors show. Wearing your insides on the outside. Never covering up who you really are. Beauty is untitled, and unnamed. It's 100 percent all-natural. Nothing added or taken away, kind of like granola. I've never compromised who I am to fit in because I've always believed in promises. The promise of a better day. The promise of a greater hope. The promise of a new tomorrow. That's why I'm beautiful: because I hope, I dream, and I know that everything will always be all right.

Emilie

ACCEPTING A NEW BODY WAS CERTAINLY TOUGH.
BUT I AM BETTER, I HAVE BEATEN THIS DISEASE,
AND NOW I KNOW WHAT BEAUTY MEANS.
I THOUGHT BEAUTY MEANT YOU HAD TO BE THIN,
BUT IN TRUTH, BEAUTY LIES BEYOND ONE'S SKIN.
WHAT MAKES ME BEAUTIFUL, WHAT DO I SAY?

karen

I THOUGHT BEAUTY MEANT YOU WERE THIN,
So I BEGAN A GAME THAT NO ONE WINS.
AT MY NINTH BIRTHDAY, I ATE NO CAKE,
BY TEN, ALL THAT MATTERED WAS MY WEIGHT.
ONE, TWO, SEVEN YEARS PASSED BY,
WHILE I COUNTED CALORIES AND SLOWLY DIED.
GRADE SCHOOL AND JUNIOR HIGH WERE FINISHED,
IN THE YEARBOOK I WAS VOTED SLIMMEST.
MY WORLD CAME TO A HALT IN HIGH SCHOOL,
I FINALLY REALIZED ANOREXIA WAS NOT COOL.
RECOVERY WAS SLOW, SETBACKS WERE ROUGH,
ACCEPTING A NEW BODY WAS CERTAINLY TOUGH.
BUT I AM BETTER, I HAVE BEATEN THIS DISEASE,
AND NOW I KNOW WHAT BEAUTY MEANS.
I THOUGHT BEAUTY MEANT YOU HAD TO BE THIN,
BUT IN TRUTH, BEAUTY LIES BEYOND ONE'S SKIN.
WHAT MAKES ME BEAUTIFUL, WHAT DO I SAY?
IT IS WHO I AM, NOT THAT I LOOK A CERTAIN WAY.
I AM BEAUTIFUL BECAUSE I UNDERSTAND CHILDREN
AND WE MAKE EACH OTHER SMILE:

  I AM BEAUTIFUL BECAUSE I HELP OTHER PEOPLE;
  I AM BEAUTIFUL BECAUSE I HAVE A LOVE FOR LIFE;
  I AM BEAUTIFUL BECAUSE I CARE ABOUT OUR WORLD;
  I AM BEAUTIFUL BECAUSE I AM ME.

laura

i never considered
myself beautiful until
i met my friends

I'm not perfect and I attend high school at a center for at-risk girls. I never considered myself beautiful until I met my friends. The friends I have at my school helped me realize that I am a caring person with a good personality. As a group we are beautiful.

I am the funny one. Selena is the player, always having a boyfriend; Jennifer, the quiet one; Lonnie, the mediator; Elizabeth, the serious one. The mother of the group is Crystal. Jo, aka Jessica, has a huge and caring heart. We have so much fun. I laugh so hard with them that my stomach aches. So many teens need to drink or get high to have fun. We have fun by just being our naturally goofy selves.

Friends who make you feel comfortable being yourself is beautiful. That's exactly how I feel, and what I am.

Bailey

My voice is high-pitched and becomes annoying. I am clumsy
and fall a lot. My legs have many scars from falling off
bikes and down stairs. The neighborhood I live in is not
the richest in town. I choose not to do drugs even though
they are around me. I am not the smartest in the class-
room. I cannot sing well but can spit rhymes better than
boys. I am beautiful because: I play sports and get sweaty
on a daily basis; my muscular thighs do not fit into size
1 jeans; I have noticeable character flaws on my face; my
hair doesn't always do what I want it to do; my mother
says so and she is always right. I am beautiful because I
say so and that's all that matters.

(My brother)   (me)

Faridah

I've been discriminated against a lot as a Black Muslim especially since 9-11. Just the other day I was online in a chat room and was appalled to see racial slurs. I was called names and was told to go **BACK TO AFRICA**. I pity them for believing that the COLOR·OF·THEIR·SKIN makes them better than me. My religion draws discrimination too. When I go to places like the Mall people give me nasty looks like I'm a mean person, or they look at me as if they're scared, like I'm a terrorist. I try to ignore them but it's hard and it makes me feel bad.

Even at my mosque, where almost everyone else is Pakistani, I experience racial backlash being one of the few black girls. I never thought this would happen to me at the mosque. We are all supposed to be equal in the sight of God.

Despite these challenges I manage to stand tall. What gets me through is my family, friends, and religion. Usually I pray to God to be strong, to show these people the truth, and to forgive them. Since all of this isn't in my hands, I don't dwell on it. I focus on my strengths and on what is true,

and I stand before GOD as an honest person.

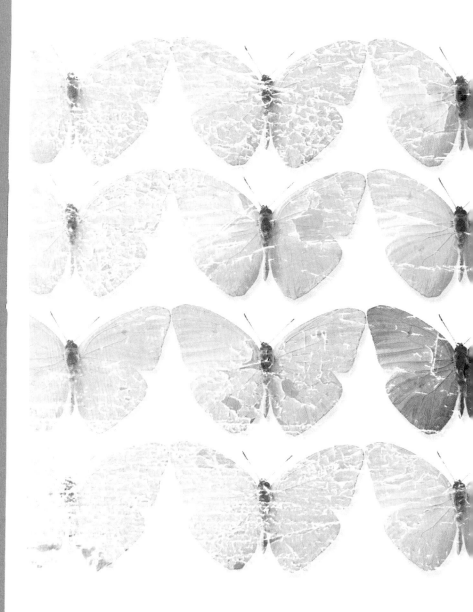

erin

Every morning and night, I looked in the mirror and would identify all of my flaws. I think that the influence of magazines that define the "norm" of what's beautiful by slender, flawless models affected the way I looked at myself. I was too skinny or too tall. Too this or too that. There was no end to finding another thing wrong about myself.

But I have come to realize my beauty through the people that I have helped- whether to carry something for them, or just to talk if they are sitting alone. It is not my outside appearance that they see. It is who I am on the inside that allows them to appreciate and respect me. I touch their lives and hearts by being myself.

I am grateful.
I am blessed.
I am beautiful.

cassie

I have many beautiful quali-
ties and interests.
One of my favorite things
is being involved with
flying horses—also known
as homing pigeons. I have
four of these graceful,
intelligent beauties, who
every morning brighten my
day. I watch the sun hit
their white wings as they
fly with such hope into the
valley and scoop back up like
a squadron into our trees.

Watching them soar into the
open morning makes me feel
such joy—as though my heart
has been set free. I express
this joy through compassion
and love during the day by
drawing, writing, and playing
soccer and musical instru-
ments.

I feel that God created everyone with her own beauty.
I am proud to say, "I am beautiful!"

I am a lucky person. I am pretty talented academically and musically. While it's a little uncomfortable, some people call me extraordinary. I, however, think that I am other-than-ordinary by an even rarer standard: I am a fourteen-year-old American girl who is perfectly satisfied with her appearance. My journey has been short in time, but I guess rather lengthy in its depth. In the five years from fourth grade to ninth, I have grown from fussing with my hair to doing what's important to me. I have gone from wishing for others to think that I am beautiful to doing things in my life that make me feel beautiful. I think if all of us stopped worrying about what others think of us and start *being* the type of person that we wish to be, we'd all exceed our expectations of *becoming* beautiful. We would be truly beautiful people because we are happy with ourselves.

lola

alexis

I am satisfied with myself. I don't have an hourglass shape or wear makeup. I like my natural look—and I am not allowed to wear makeup anyway! When I look in the mirror, I can see past my pimples, glasses, and oversized teeth. What I see is my toffee-colored complexion, my round full lips, and chocolate-brown hair. I see a young, black, studious girl who is trying to make a difference in the world.

One certain beauty trait of mine is that I have a fiery passion that motivates me always to try my best.

I am beautiful because

am satisfied with myself

beauty is distributed throughout my body, inherited from my mother and grandmothers. Beauty is a strong sense of love and that is a gift that I have been given by my family. My friends express love towards me too. Those who love me have taught me the true properties of beauty, and I reflect them.

One of my teachers said that I wasn't a crowd-pleaser. She meant that I am not here to live up to others' expectations, but only to my own. My standards are to do what I feel is right while upholding my unique style.

Beauty is distributed
throughout my body
inherited from my mother and
grandmother. Beauty is a
strong ... of love and
that is ... that I have
been given ... my family. My
friends ... love towards
me too ... and love me
have taught me the true
properties of beauty, and I
reflect ...

One of my teachers said that
I wasn't a crowd-pleaser.
She meant that I am not here
to live up to others
expectations but only to my
own. My ... are to do
what I ...

The best and most ...
world cannot be ... even ...
must be felt with the ...

lucie

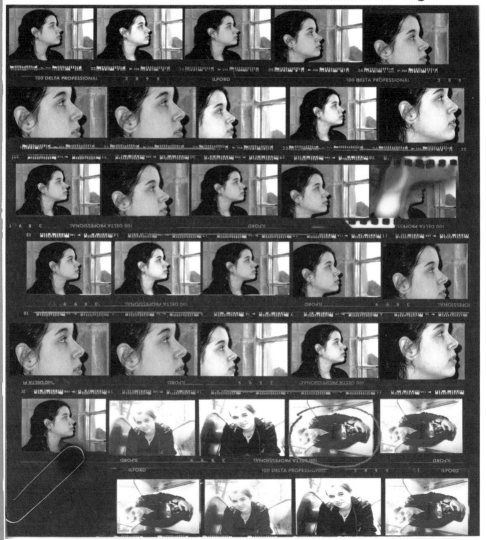

I love to show people the world in a different light. With a camera, I can transform an everyday object into an image that people react to. I like it when someone looks at a picture I have created and is affected by it. When I see a person deep in thought over one of my photos, I like to think that perhaps, without even knowing it, her perspective is changed.

Elise

above all i accept myself

michelle

I accept myself for who I am. I may not be perfect, but I think I am kind of wonderful and extraordinary. My morals are strong and I know the impact that I want to make on the world. I don't let people bring me into a place that I don't want to be. While I respect the points of view of others—my family, friends, even my enemies or just acquaintances—I don't let anyone sway my beliefs. I choose my friends because they are nice, intelligent, and fun. I don't go after the popular group just to be classified as one of them. I am wild and crazy to a certain extent, and at the appropriate time. I don't show off for attention.

I have learned what beauty is from struggling with an eating disorder for two years. For me, it is being myself and not being afraid to stand out. It is not being afraid to be first and to show what I feel and to share my thoughts with others.

There is so much more to life than worrying about what everyone else might think of your body. And the effort it takes to do that hurts. Eating disorders only give sadness and pain. One of my good friends died from anorexia at age nineteen—doing the ultimate harm to herself and causing others much pain as well. I have gone through inpatient treatment and more therapy than I like to remember. Sometimes I want to go back to my old habits, but then I recall how much I have put into my recovery. I want to keep living. I want to dance, do gymnastics, finish high school, and most of all, have fun. I am making a choice to recover.

My beauty comes from within. I could be the most beautiful person in the world, but that doesn't matter because external beauty fades. When it is gone, all that is left is what's inside. I refuse to cause myself any more pain for someone else's view of me. Love me or hate me, I am my own person.

Lisa
i have learned what beauty is

★ katie ★

Beauty confuses me.
Who's to decide the answer to this question?

Beauty Confuses Me

Is it being rich? Or showing lots of booty?
Who's to decide the answer to this question?
People's 25 Hottest Stars have lied.
For it isn't your body or makeup or hair
or who you're with or what you wear.
What matters is what's inside your heart
It's what's in there that sets you apart.
If some were stripped of material things,
of makeup, designer clothes, and diamond rings
what would be left but naked souls
leaving some certainly as ugly as trolls.
Take all that away and I'd still be pretty
because I'm honest, most sincere, and witty.
I know what makes me beautiful too:
my self-confidence makes my person true.
My truth to myself sets me apart.
I know who I am deep in my heart.
My outlook on life is a beautiful thing,
a smile to your face it could certainly bring!
We're only on Earth for a little while,
so why not live life with a beautiful smile?

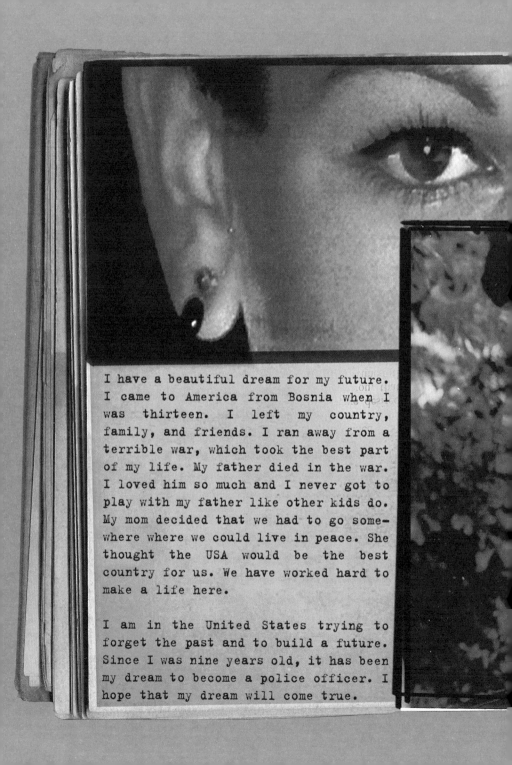

I have a beautiful dream for my future. I came to America from Bosnia when I was thirteen. I left my country, family, and friends. I ran away from a terrible war, which took the best part of my life. My father died in the war. I loved him so much and I never got to play with my father like other kids do. My mom decided that we had to go somewhere where we could live in peace. She thought the USA would be the best country for us. We have worked hard to make a life here.

I am in the United States trying to forget the past and to build a future. Since I was nine years old, it has been my dream to become a police officer. I hope that my dream will come true.

Dzevada

Unlike lots of girls, I don't let it go to my head when people tell me that I am beautiful. Unlike too many girls, I don't sleep around to be popular. I am beautiful and I am popular. But for different reasons.

I am popular because I do community service, and I am involved in lots of clubs and after-school activities. I never get into fights because I don't have any enemies.

I am beautiful because I care about people. Whether young or old, black or white, everyone deserves respect. I accept everyone even if they are different from me. I love children and I think the elderly are so adorable and lucky to have made it so far in life. Stephanie

I am at peace with myself, because I know that I am the best that I can be. I am happy about the gifts I was given. Many people dislike their lives and you can see it in their every motion and action. If you are happy about the blessings bestowed on you, it reflects out to others. I make a choice to be happy and feel how much of a blessing this journey is.

I do sports—they make me more confident and interesting. I have a fun personality that makes me beautiful; the feelings of having fun and being fun are a real reward. This year, I am trying something new—my brother and I are going to be homeschooled by my dad.

Beauty can be found anywhere; mine is found in the way I love life.

teale

There was a time when I thought nothing was beautiful. I hated myself, the world, and everything in it, and to show it, I frequently cut and starved myself. I don't know exactly why it started, but I was suffering from depression and dealing with many problems. I felt that I just couldn't talk about things to anyone. I felt that I deserved punishment. When I started at my college (the British version of American high school), I met a beautiful person named Alyson, who became my friend. She started to show me the little things in the world that mattered and she taught me to believe in myself and my future. Thanks to her patience, encouragement, and support, two years later I am happy, alive, and about to start my courses at university. I have learned to find pleasure and beauty in the little things that make our lives worth living. Everyday I wake up and smile because I now can experience what before was lost. I can hear the birds and see the sunshine. I can write letters that flow from me, and draw original pictures. I can feel an animal's fur, sense its breathing under soft skin. When I hug someone I feel eyelashes brush my cheek, their love and warmth. I can smell flowers, freshly baked cookies, morning rain, and salty sea-spray. I listen to my favorite song and how each single note makes up a tune; every part merging into that one sound which makes me smile inside. I think everyone is like the notes in a favorite song: pretty on our own, but if we work together and support each other we can make something that is truly beautiful. I am beautiful because like everyone else, I am an individual who has the power to help change another's life for the better.

katy

brittany

Not one person in this world needs to enlighten me to the fact that I am beautiful. Many years of training in Taekwondo have taught me to fully accept myself. I am confident, assured, and self-reliant. No one is able to eradicate my spirit and morals.

My intellect further makes me who I am. Far beyond just "book smarts," I encompass common sense. Comprehension of clear life objectives far surpasses anything a textbook could teach.

I might put on makeup and spend hours messing with my hair, but it's my personality, attitude, self-assurance, and intelligence that constitute me—the beautiful young woman that I know I am.

I do my own thing. I don't wait around for guys to call. If they don't call, then so be it. I have better things to do with my time than sit around and wait or complain. I want to have fun and feel good wherever I go, whatever I do. My friends and I love surfing because not a lot of girls do it. It's a great feeling—one you don't get very often. When you finally get up and you are standing on the board, riding a wave, you feel like you are floating, but you are going fast. It's scary, but a good scary.

I also play soccer and tennis. I do sports year-round because if I didn't, I wouldn't be able to focus at all. I'd just be on the phone all the time and not doing my homework. Sports definitely keep me on track. I didn't think that I would ever say that, but it's true.

CAMILLE

dreamer, poet, future doctor, best friend, leader

artist, daughter, student, photographer, friend, actress, sister,

sally

I Have Always Been The Different Child

Even as a little girl, I dressed and
acted differently than other children.
It didn't matter, though, just as
long as I was nice to them and they
were nice to me.

In middle school, I wasn't the most
popular girl or the best dressed, but
I was voted "Best Friend." To me, that
title is a thousand times more
important than any other.

My grandma used to always say, "Pretty
is as pretty does." I think about this
every day when I leave the house. My
goal is to be that pretty person, to
show people that my actions and
optimistic personality make me pretty.
No outfit or coat of makeup could ever
do that. Beauty is beyond the physical.
Once we realize that, we will also
realize that we are all beautiful.
If we are constantly true to ourselves,
nothing can go wrong.

I live atop my own little mountain, where I am truly beautiful! I got here with the help of my great parents who created the opportunity for me to live all over the United States and to learn about everything that this great country has to offer. I live one day at a time and cherish every moment. I don't worry about what everyone is wearing, what's in style, or how my hair looks. I only worry about being the best I can be at every given moment.

I am energetic, lively, and confident. My loud personality silences every storm. Beautiful is being true to yourself and fulfilling your dreams. I love being me. No one tells me how to live my life and, on my mountain, I never let anyone bring me down.

Aimee Frances

Lindsay

Like a video game, I feel like we are living in a world where nothing is real. Filled with obsessions of being thin; fashion magazines dictating what's in and what's hot; extravagant, expensive procedures to preserve or create "beautiful" people, women and girls have been beguiled to believe that we have nothing to offer if we do not look a certain way.

It's understandable that people want to see beautiful things, things that attract their eyes and exhilarate their senses. But our fascination with the superficial is robbing us of just that. Truly beautiful women are everywhere, but they are walking in the shadow of our culture's beauty ideal. Believe me, there are many intelligent, caring women teaching girls what it means to be beautiful: being truthful and not feeling obligated to be something you're not.

If we could stop being afraid of who we really are, then we will see the real beauty in ourselves. This is what I try to remember, and it makes me feel beautiful.

melissa

beautiful soul

While most of my peers are studying how to get that flawless Britney body, or how to walk like J.Lo, I am busy working on myself.
Who am I?
A talented writer; an excellent artist; an awesome biblical historian; a good friend; a compassionate caregiver; an intelligent student. While others may copycat celebrities, I know that appearance is only the external part of my grand makeup.

My beautiful soul is inside and protected from the movie and magazine brainwashing aimed at my generation of girls.

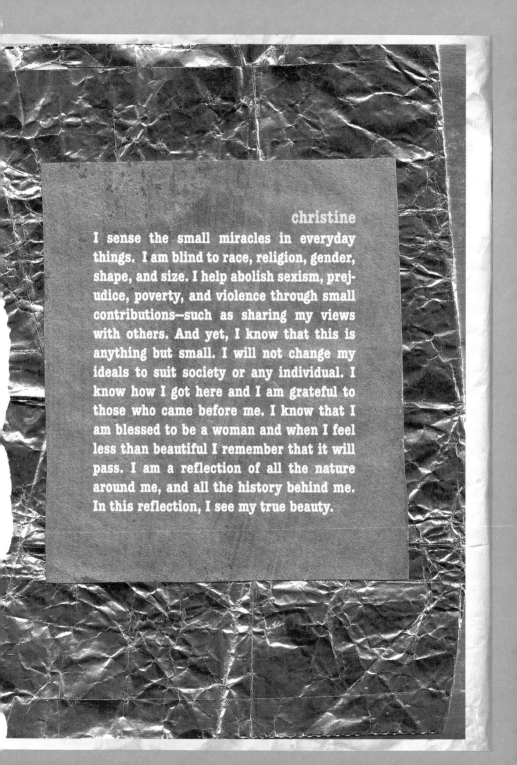

christine

I sense the small miracles in everyday things. I am blind to race, religion, gender, shape, and size. I help abolish sexism, prejudice, poverty, and violence through small contributions—such as sharing my views with others. And yet, I know that this is anything but small. I will not change my ideals to suit society or any individual. I know how I got here and I am grateful to those who came before me. I know that I am blessed to be a woman and when I feel less than beautiful I remember that it will pass. I am a reflection of all the nature around me, and all the history behind me. In this reflection, I see my true beauty.

Amber Nicole

I am beautiful.
I'm not conceited or full of myself.
Rather the contrary, I confess.
It's not my appearance that makes me pretty.
About my body image, I refuse to obsess.

I am beautiful.
I am a Christian and I strive to do good.
In the school orchestra, I play the violin.
I enjoy sports, but I'm not very good.
And I understand the purpose is not to win.

I am beautiful.
My sister is my best friend and always will be.
I love her unconditionally, and she the same.
She helps me from day to day.
She's the reason for what I became.

I am beautiful.
No matter what you may perceive
I know this to be the truth.
I am lucky to know this
in the challenging years of youth.

It's so important to be open-minded. If you're not, you'll miss out on a lot. You can't judge people by their looks or decide that you have your little group of friends and don't have to get to know other people. People say that I am bubbly and, sometimes, too outgoing. But I am always meeting really great, interesting people and learning from them. If you are sitting next to someone and you get the vibe to say hi, do it. You might make a new friend.

*LAUREN

Antonia

My beauty is so much more than
words can describe. For beauty
is not merely what others see
with the eye. It starts from
within, inside the soul unseen.

Too long the world has given
distorted views. Beauty is an
ideal too narrow and misused.
Let's try to change the beauty
misconception. We must stop the
world's mass deception.

What makes me beautiful? Is it
the way I look? The way I feel?
Is it defined in a book? Is my
beauty real?

I know what makes me beautiful.
It is the way I treat everyone.
It is my personality. It is the
great things I have done. It is
why others want to know me.

I am an Activist.
I am Blunt.
I am a Child.

I am Dangerous.
I am Eclectic.
I am Frank.

I am still Growing.
I am a Humanist.
I am Intellectual.
I am Juvenile.
I am Kinetic. ~
I am Lonely.
I am Melodramatic.
I am a Nonconformist.
I am Opinionated.
I am a Poet.
I am Quiet.
I am Romantic.
I am Spirited.
I am a Threat.
I am Unique.
I am a Virgin.

theresa

I am a Woman.
I am the X-Chromosome.
I am Young.
I am Zealous.
I am Beautiful.

I am me.
I am a teenager
attempting to live
each day, *LOUDLY*.
Making noise and
breaking barriers.
Holding the hand of
the girl who walks beside
me, inside me.

Walking on.
Walking forward.
Continuing to live
as a blend:
Hot~Cold
Young~Old

A Girl ~ A Woman.

I am beautiful because . . .

On this page, you are invited to create your own G—LYSTE in a style that matches your unique personality.

SO WHAT'S A G—LYSTE?

G—LYSTE is an expression of a girl's beauty, inside out. Hence, the word STYLE turned inside out... LYSTE. (G for Girl, of course!) G—LYSTE does more than just list your special characteristics. Through your words and your art, it forms a deeper, more meaningful expression of your own unique style and beauty.

Make as many as you wish. Make one with your friends. Make one for your friends. Or make a private one just for you. As with all art, there are no rules, except that a G—LYSTE should have your photo, your words, and colors that celebrate the deepest essence of you. Most important, it should complete the powerful assertion, "I am beautiful because..." And whether a hundred people see it, or only you, know that it's the truth because it came from you.

Have fun, and be beautiful!

The ABCs of Feeling Beautiful

An A–Z Guide for Naming, Claiming, and Living Your True Beauty

A

ACKNOWLEDGE AND AFFIRM . Acknowledge your right to define beauty on your own terms. This is the first step in affirming your beauty, and shunning the rather ridiculous ideal of the popular culture. Create literal affirmations that support your new way of thinking about yourself: "I am kind." " I am passionate." "I am beautiful when I _____." (Fill in the blank and sing your praises!)

B

BE your BEST. It gets hard to know what your best is when you are overly infatuated with celebrities and overexposed to advertisements promising perfection. But being your best is good enough, and when you decide that this is true, then pride, satisfaction, and pleasure will replace comparing yourself to others.

C

Don't COMPARE and CRITICIZE. That's right! Don't compare yourself—any part of yourself—to others, most especially to models and actresses. You can't win this one. Nobody can. Recognize that the average fashion model is five to six inches taller and weighs thirty to forty pounds less than the average American woman! This is the truth! Also, stop criticizing yourself. Try it for a day, then a week, then a month. Pick a day to put a rubber band on your wrist and (gently) snap it against your skin every time you let a critical thought go through your mind. (This will get your attention and let you know how much you criticize yourself!) Then remember to replace negative messages with positive ones.

D

DEFINE your beauty for yourself. Start at the top of your head and work all the way down to your toes. What parts of your body do you like, are special, serve you with health and strength, remind you of a loved family member? Look within. Mentally explore who you are and what unique things you bring to this world. What are your talents? Accomplishments? Dreams? Write your answers down. Put the paper in a place where you will see it from time to time.

E

EXERCISE and EAT Well. Sensible, regular exercise and healthy eating are the two essential ingredients to help you feel and look your best. The benefits of physical fitness and team sports provide a powerful combination for building self-esteem. Team sports are not your thing? That's okay, just get moving! Build your own team of several friends to challenge and inspire each other to healthy amounts of exercise on a regular basis. Combine exercise with a well-balanced diet of healthy foods, while limiting junk foods, and your strong and vital body will remind you every day how beautiful you are.

F

FOCUS on the positive. The power of positive thinking is much more than a cliché. Its benefits are seen and practiced the world over. Tap into your personal well of mental and physical health by steering clear of critical thoughts. Instead, repeat positive thoughts in your mind about your beautiful self. Create your own personal mantra—a private declaration that you repeat to yourself at least once a day. Something like: "I am strong, healthy, and glowing." "My happiness is a reflection of my lively spirit and love of life." "I have strength, stamina, power, and purpose." Come up with your own positive thoughts, but just think of something!

G

GET ●ut! Solitude has its place; alone time is important for everyone. But hiding out in the house is a bad idea. Get out and enjoy life. Go places and see new things. This will help you to build a positive mental outlook and feel good about yourself.

H

HAPPINESS. You deserve to feel happy! We all have to deal with problems, but worrying about physical appearance doesn't have to be one of them. Go back and read through the essays in this book. Learn from the many girls who wrote about their identity being more—much more—than what they look like. The key to happiness, and beauty, is found in taking pleasure and participating in life.

I

IMAGINE. Imagine your life as you would like it to be, with everything going really great. What are your dreams? What does your future hold? How would you like the day before you to play out? Putting a clear thought in your mind is the first step to creating that reality. How could it be otherwise? You have to think of something before it can be born into existence.

J

JUDGE ʀ●t. Judging is a full-time job that leads nowhere. When judging starts, it is hard to stop. So, don't do it. Don't do it to yourself, and don't do to others. It is harmful and hurtful. Everyone deserves not to be judged at a first glance—including you. When judging thoughts come up, switch them to complimentary ones that acknowledge the good and positive in yourself and others.

K

KICK the diet habit. Diets, per se, don't work and can lead to serious health consequences. Most diet plans and aids are like lots of other products—things companies sell to make money. The diet business is estimated to be around a $40 billion a year industry. If diets worked, then why are Americans becoming more overweight every year? A healthy, fit body is realized only through reasonable exercise and healthy eating. Check with your health professional to learn what that means for you and your body type.

L

LISTS. Make them. Make a list of five physical features of yours that you like and appreciate, and why. Then make another list of the five personality traits that you like about yourself, and why. Move on to a list of five things that you are grateful for. Finally, make a list of five achievements that you are particularly proud of. Do this exercise once a month until the items on the lists become the first things you think of when describing yourself.

M

MEDIA smarts. Consciously think about what is being said and sold in the advertising and media images you see. Acknowledge that models and movie stars don't represent reality. Recognize that their images are retouched or fixed by a computer to look a certain way. Be aware that many advertising messages are specifically designed to make you feel inferior so that you will buy the advertised product.

N

NURTURE. Nurture positive thoughts in others. Respond to your friends thoughtfully when they criticize themselves. Don't let their negative remarks go unchallenged. Rather, tell them why their statements are untrue and self-defeating. You admire and respect your close friends, right?

Well, they feel the same way toward you. Your statements stopping their self-criticism will be heard, and your effort will make a difference.

O

OUT! Out with your scale—beauty is not measured in pounds. Out with fashion magazines, until you are able to read them while keeping a critical eye toward the editorial and advertising gimmicks. Out with that pair of old blue jeans in the back of your closet that doesn't fit and screams "failure" every time you try them on. Out with products that are shamefully advertised to make you feel inferior. Out with the lies and notions that your beauty is based on your outside appearance alone.

P

PICK healthy relationships. Pick friends and romantic partners who help you to feel and support your sense of beauty. Don't hang out with people who belittle you and criticize your physical appearance. Anyone who does this has an agenda other than friendship and love. You should be able to count on those closest to you for help and encouragement to be your unique best—not someone or something else.

Q

QUESTION everything. Question the motives behind a company's promise in an advertised message. Question a magazine's intention to "authoritatively" write a story that subtly supports advertisers' products. Raise the question why a "friend" at school would always put you down. Query others about their experiences and thoughts about the beauty culture in order to keep the conversation on this subject going. Above all, ask yourself how you want to spend this one precious life you have: feeling beautiful, or not?

R

ROLE MODEL for others. Positive role modeling for children, younger girls, and friends is an important undertaking for turning the tide of self-defeating behavior. Realize that constant talk about calorie-counting, diet, exercise, and imperfections is heard and learned. This is so common that it has become an activity of social interaction between girls, little different from discussing school assignments or the upcoming weekend. Cancel it off of your to-do list!

S

Be SHAME-FREE. All of the insanity revolving around beauty issues leaves many feeling shameful for not measuring up to the arbitrary standards before them. Do you know anyone who can control naturally the length of their legs, how straight their hair is, or the color of their eyes? So why subject yourself to the same crazy scale? Let go of the thought that you are a success or a failure based on comparing yourself to a false ideal.

T

TREAT yourself to nice things that make you feel beautiful. From time to time, buy yourself something special that accentuates one of your favorite features—a new tube of lipstick, earrings, a cool baseball cap, or a hip-hugging belt. Adorn the glamorous, sassy, and individual features of your unique beauty.

U

UNDERSTAND what's going on. Understand the pervasiveness of the media in American culture and its impact on your frame of mind. Estimates vary, but on average, you are exposed to up to six hundred advertising messages, images, and logos every single day—and about one-third of these is beauty- or diet-related. Consider that by the time you are eighteen years old, you have likely seen around one million (often distorted) "beauty" messages. Ouch!

V

VITAL interests. What is most important to you? Most enjoyable? Most satisfying? Would you exchange your family for a new eye color? Give up your favorite sport or leisure activity to be taller? Of course not. Give a moment from time to time to focus on what really brings depth and richness to your life. It is unlikely that it has anything to do with your physical appearance.

W

WATCH WHAT you WEAR. Wear clothes that you feel comfortable in and that express your own particular style and taste. There are enough fashion choices and types of stores around today to be able to meet every person's preference and pocketbook. Also, feel free to wear as little or as much makeup as you like.

X

X-PRESS yourself! Be true to who you really are while adopting, implementing, exploring, embracing, and X-pressing many of the ideas, tips, and practices from above. There is no limit to the ways you can convey your beautiful individuality.

Y

YOU. On this subject, in this case, "it" *is* all about you. It is you and your heart that matter. It is your values and how to express them that need to rise above the clutter and clatter as you make your way in this crazy culture of ours. Take the pieces of fun, fashion, and frivolity that are best for you, and leave the rest.

Z

ZERO in. Zero in on what makes you feel beautiful and happy. Live your life by what is true for you. You need no other measure of your worth.

Acknowledgments

Above all, I want to acknowledge the young women who stepped up to share their stories for this book. I hope you recognize that your courage to do so serves as inspiration for others to contemplate their own beauty and self-worth.

My profound thanks go to the many people who believed in the importance of this book, people who care about young women and know that they deserve to feel as beautiful as they really are. I acknowledge the numerous parents, teachers, and mentors of girls who helped make this book a reality for the young women they love—and those they don't even know.

As always, I thank my dear family—those who live in my home, down the street, or many miles away—for their continued support and love.

I extend a special thanks to graphic designer Anne LoCascio at Sourcebooks for the many hours she spent refining and revealing the visual beauty of this book.

And, to Deb—I look forward to a future that promises to be even more colorful and magical than our past.

About the Editor

Woody Winfree credits a college professor that she had at age nineteen as the first person to encourage her to use words for a powerful purpose. Up to that point, most adults she knew were more likely to tell her to "keep a lid on it," "quiet down," or "speak like a lady!" Since that point, however, Woody has been shaping ideas through written and spoken language to solve problems, take a stand, even effect social change. She drew on her years working in television and print journalism, magazine publishing, advertising sales, and public speaking to create the multifaceted *I Am Beautiful Project*. Through her books and other vehicles, this project is dedicated to creating a world in which every woman and girl can proudly proclaim, "I Am Beautiful!"

For more information on celebrating your beauty,
visit www.iambeautiful.com.

Woody Winfree, surrounded by two of her favorite girls—one currently a teen, one a bit past teenhood—her beautiful daughters, Romy (left) and Layla.